Tend the Body Like a Garden

Dr. Yi Song

ISBN: 979-8-9948506-5-7 (print)

This is Book Four of

Regeneration Effect :

Sacred Wisdom for Staying Young

4

Just as no two gardens are the same, no two bodies are the same. One garden may thrive in full sun with dry soil; another needs shade, rich compost, and constant moisture. Try watering a cactus like a fern and you'll see the problem immediately. But when it comes to our health, we often forget this simple truth. We follow generic advice,

one-size-fits-all programs, and influencer

trends without pausing to ask:

What does my body actually need?

Your body, like a garden, has a **unique**

terrain. A personal constitution that determines how it reacts to food, stress, sleep, climate, and aging.

Understanding that terrain is the foundation for real, long-term vitality.

From the moment you're born, your body has a natural constitution that determines how it **processes food, handles stress, and responds to different environments**. In this section, you'll begin to recognize your own constitution and how it impacts your health.

Think of constitution as your body's operating system. **Some people run hot.** Their faces flush easily, they sweat profusely, and they crave cold drinks even in winter. **Others run cold.** They bundle up in summer, their hands and feet are perpetually icy, and they can't digest raw foods without feeling bloated.

Some bodies hold onto moisture like a sponge. These people feel heavy, sluggish, and often struggle with weight gain or water retention. **Others are dry** as autumn leaves.

Their skin cracks, their joints ache, and they need constant hydration just to feel normal.

These aren't flaws or problems to fix.

They're simply **different types of gardens** requiring different care.

Mental and Physical Health Are Intertwined

Your physical health mirrors your **emotional state**. Chronic perfectionism? It often shows up as neck tension or digestive rigidity.

Long-term stress? It can weaken immunity, disturb hormones, and lead to insomnia.

I once had a client who struggled with chronic fatigue. She had seen every specialist, done every lab. Physically, nothing was "wrong." But emotionally? She was exhausted from **trying to be everything for everyone**. A mother, wife, manager, caretaker. The moment she acknowledged her emotional depletion, her physical energy began to return.

Athletes provide another clear example.

Olympic-level swimmers like Michael

Phelps, runners like Kelly Holmes, and elite

cyclists like Gunn-Rita Dahle have all

demonstrated that overtraining, constant performance pressure, and physical overexertion can lead to severe mental and physical health problems—depression, anxiety, chronic fatigue, and long-term injury. These aren't isolated incidents—they highlight a universal truth:

The human body and mind have limits, and even extreme talent or success doesn't remove them.

Our bodies and nervous systems are constantly sending signals about overload: fatigue, inflammation, pain, digestive issues, or emotional instability. Ignoring these signals—or pushing through in the name of career, image, or ambition—can have lasting consequences. Celebrities might have resources, medical support, and visibility, but they are still bound by biology.

Understanding your health means seeing both the forest and the trees—the big picture and the small, intricate pieces that make you who you are. Your body isn't just a reflection of what you eat or how much you exercise; it's an ongoing story shaped by generations before you and the choices you make every day.

Aging and the Body's Natural Waste System

As we age, the body's ability to clear waste —through lymph, digestion, breath, and sweat— slows down. Toxins begin to accumulate, leading to symptoms like joint pain, autoimmune flares, or foggy thinking.

Think of it like a river. When we're young, the current is strong.

Debris gets swept away quickly. But as we age, the flow slows. Sediment builds up. Blockages form. What once moved freely now stagnates.

This is why we see a rise in interest around treatments like **plasma exchange**, fasting, or detoxes. But without a **strong immune foundation**, those treatments are like pulling weeds while ignoring the depleted soil. True longevity requires supporting the whole system.

Nourishing the gut, calming the nervous system, clearing stagnation, and allowing the body to do what it was designed to do: self-heal.

You've probably heard the phrase: *"Health begins in the gut."* It's true. But not in the way most people think.

Many turn to **probiotic supplements** as a quick fix, but gut health isn't about one pill. It's about **ecosystem diversity**. And that requires lifestyle, not just capsules.

The real secret isn't about defying age; it's about *harmonizing* with it.

Supporting the body's natural rhythms, replenishing what's been lost, and **slowing the decline rather than chasing an illusion.**

When you stop fighting the process and start working with it, you realize that aging isn't the enemy. It's simply evolution—an invitation to live with greater awareness, intention, and vitality than ever before.

Instead of focusing on unattainable immortality, this chapter guides you to:

- **Accept your body's natural limitations** while working to strengthen and optimize your constitution.

- **Embrace longevity strategies** that slow decline without denying the reality of aging.

- **Shift the goal** from endless life to a full, vibrant, and meaningful one.

Take digestive problems, for example. The

root cause is often not physical at all, but

emotional stress.

 Stress acts like a drought in the garden—it

dries up the irrigation system, blocks the

natural flow, and leaves the soil depleted.

The bloating or indigestion you feel are just the visible weeds; the real issue lies deeper in the roots.

Your body is a holographic system —every part reflects the whole.

When you nourish one area, you're supporting the entire ecosystem.

Healing, then, isn't about treating an isolated symptom.

It's about restoring the flow of energy through the garden.

I've seen this truth in my own body. I have a predisposition to coughing. For years, I treated it the Western way—with antibiotics and cough medicine—assuming it was an infection in the lungs or throat. But Traditional Chinese Medicine taught me to look deeper. The cough wasn't coming from the lungs at all—it was a signal of weakness in my kidney energy.

In Chinese medicine, **the kidney anchors the body's energy,** guiding it downward. When that energy weakens, the lung energy can't descend properly. Instead of flowing down, it rises—causing the cough, or even acid reflux. The problem isn't just in the respiratory system; it's in the garden's irrigation.

To heal, you don't just cut the weeds—you nourish the roots, clear the flow, and guide the energy back down where it belongs.

Because even the most beautifully designed system becomes blocked when overburdened.

Stress. Emotional buildup. Toxins. Over-scheduling. Repressed grief. Unprocessed trauma. Poor sleep. Overexposure to technology.

All of these cause **energetic stagnation**—leading to inflammation, mental fog, anxiety, insomnia, digestive issues, chronic fatigue, and more.

A reset isn't a luxury —it's essential maintenance for your system.

In Daoism, this restoration is called **wu wei** —often translated as "effortless action." It's not laziness or apathy. It's the elegant understanding that sometimes the most powerful action... is stillness.

When you slow down:

· Your **Qi begins to move again**

· Your digestion becomes more efficient

· Your thoughts become clearer

· Your breath deepens

· Your body starts remembering how to heal

When you create space, you reconnect with

your **internal compass**. You stop reacting

from stress, and you start responding from clarity.

There's an inspirational video where a group of scientists **injected adrenaline into trees** that were in their natural winter dormancy—a slowed, restorative metabolic state. The idea was to see if they could keep the forest "awake" and productive year-round. At first, nothing looked unusual. But slowly, the trees began to weaken. Without their seasonal rest, their systems couldn't recalibrate.

Eventually, they died.

That experiment revealed something simple but profound:

Every living thing on this planet needs a break.

We forget that sometimes. It's hard to rest when there are bills to pay, deadlines to meet, families to care for, or ambitions to chase. The world rewards momentum, not stillness. But nature shows us a different

rhythm. Even the most resilient trees, the ones that survive for centuries, surrender to seasons of dormancy.

They don't fight the winter; they trust it.

That might sound counterintuitive in a culture that idolizes speed, hustle, and relentless productivity. We grow up hearing that pushing harder is the only way forward —that discomfort is a badge of honor and rest is something you earn, not something you inherently need. We're told to override signals, suppress fatigue, and "power through" as if the body were a machine rather than a living, responsive ecosystem.

But nature doesn't operate that way.

Nature doesn't heal through force —it heals through flow.

Water doesn't carve canyons by slamming into rock; it reshapes the world through steady, rhythmic persistence. Plants don't grow because someone yanks them toward the sun; they unfurl on their own timeline.

Even seasons understand this: winter retreats

not because spring fights it, but because the natural cycle allows the shift.

Your healing works exactly the same way.

Recovery doesn't start with friction, resistance, or willpower—it begins with allowing. When you stop fighting your body and start listening to it, you give it permission to recalibrate. When you slow down, breathe, and create stillness, you open up the internal space where repair can happen. Rest isn't passive; it's one of the most active biological states your body enters. Hormones rebalance. Inflammation lowers. Neural pathways reset. Cells detoxify and rebuild.

This pause you take—the moment of stepping back from doing—isn't the opposite of progress.

It *is* the mechanism of progress.

The more you pause and return to center, the more

effective your actions

become.

Practical Reset Rituals

Resetting doesn't always require a dramatic retreat or a week off. Often, the most powerful resets happen in **micro-moments** —small shifts that realign your energy, clarity, and nervous system. Below are simple rituals you can return to again and again.

Breath Reset

Your breath is the fastest way to shift your nervous system out of stress mode and into calm. Even just **3 minutes** can transform your inner state.

Try this: Sit quietly. Inhale for 4 → Hold for 4 → Exhale for 6. Repeat this for 6 rounds. Let the breath lengthen naturally.

Sleep Reset

One night of deep, unbroken sleep can restore more than a week of stressed-out productivity. Rest isn't a luxury. It's your birthright.

Try this:

· Power down all screens at least two hours
before bed.

· Lay on your back and try *legs-up-the-wall*
pose for 10 minutes.

· Sip a warm, calming tea like **chamomile**,
tulsi, or **reishi**.

· Give yourself permission to **fully rest**—
without needing to "earn it."

Nutrition Reset

When your digestion is off, your mood, energy, and focus all follow. Your gut is your **second brain**—and it needs simplicity to heal.

Try this:

· For 2–3 days, eat simple, nourishing meals: Soups, congee, warm cooked vegetables, bone broth.

· Avoid raw, cold, or complex meals that stress your digestive fire.

· Add warming herbs like **ginger**,
cinnamon, and **fennel** to support gut
balance.

Mental Reset

Mental clutter drains your energy just like
physical exhaustion. Unspoken worries,
looping thoughts, and inner criticism create
invisible weight.

Try this:

· Write one full page answering: *"What am I*

holding onto that I'm ready to release?"

· Speak out loud what you're thinking—
naming it gives it less power.

· Visualize your mind like a clear sky,
watching thoughts float by like passing
clouds.

Qi Reset

Energy (Qi) flows like water. If it gets
blocked, symptoms appear: fatigue, pain,
brain fog, or emotional swings. QiGong and
movement help restore flow.

Try this:

· Practice gentle QiGong for 10 minutes—morning or evening. Movements like **"Swimming Dragon"**, **"Spinal Shake"**, or **"Cloud Hands"** are beautiful places to start.

· Even a simple **walking meditation** or slow, rhythmic breathing outdoors resets your inner terrain.

Tending the body like a garden starts with daily simple routines for the skin, the cellular health and the circulation in the

body.

If you would like more personalized advice on how to tend your particular garden, please scan the QR code for more information to preorder "Regeneration Effect: Sacred Wisdom for Staying Young" and learn how you can implement all the principles in your life.

ABOUT THE AUTHOR

Dr. Yi Song was born and raised in Beijing, China, into a family with seventeen generations of experience in both Chinese and Western medicine. Twenty-eight years ago, she came to the United States to study pathology at Brown University. After observing the shortcomings of symptom-focused treatments, Dr. Song returned to her roots to focus on true regenerative healing — addressing disease at its source. She has had a holistic clinic in Boston since 2004. In

2018, she founded the Zenerchi Retreat in Medellin, Colombia. Her introduction to stem cell therapy in 2020 was marked by her mother's successful treatment and subsequent independence at age 81. Dr. Song believes that stem cell therapy aligns with holistic principles and is the author of "Regeneration Effect: Sacred Wisdom for Staying Young" and the series of seven books in "The Six Principles to Natural Longevity". Her vision is to combine stem cell therapy, Traditional Chinese Medicine, and anti-aging treatments to help people live a long, high-quality life. She offers advanced stem cell treatments at Zenerchi Retreat in Colombia not available in the US. You can also get consultation about your conditions and concerns in person in Boston or at our network of doctors in the US and online.